# Chapter 10
# Using Natural Resources

## You Will Discover

- what natural resources are.
- which energy sources are renewable and which are nonrenewable.
- how we can conserve energy.

**Web Games**
Take It to the Net
pearsonsuccessnet.com

online
**Student Edition**
pearsonsuccessnet.com

# How can living things always have the natural resources they need?

solar energy

ore

petroleum

fossil fuels

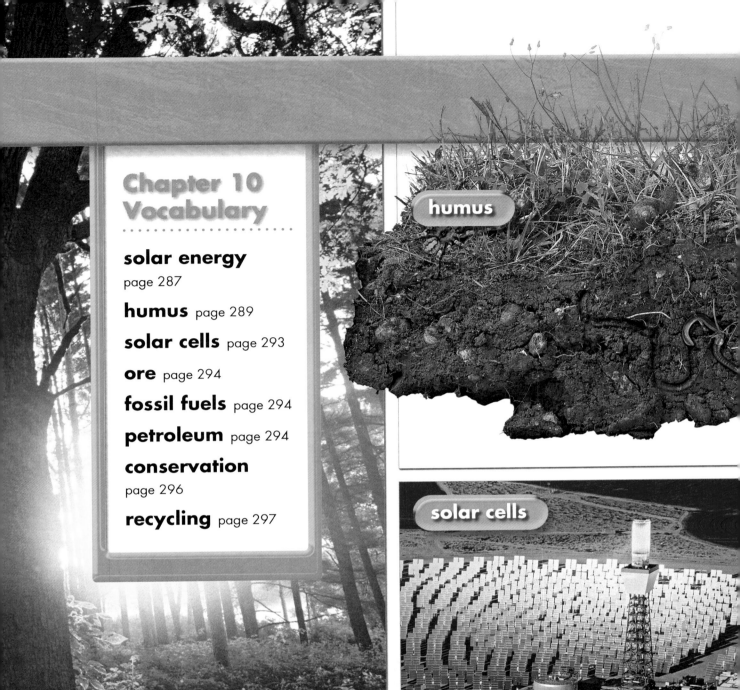

# Chapter 10 Vocabulary

humus

solar cells

conservation

Conservation means using only what you need as efficiently as possible.

recycling

## Explore How can you collect sunlight?

**Materials**

round-bottom bowl

aluminum foil

$\frac{1}{2}$ stick of clay

2 thermometers

tape

clock with a second hand
(or timer or stopwatch)

**Process Skills**

You made **inferences** based on your **measurements**.

**What to Do**

1 Line the bowl with foil. If needed, use loops of tape to hold the foil on the bowl.

2 Tilt the bowl so the Sun shines into it. Use clay to hold the bowl in place

Use clay to prop up one thermometer.

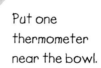

Put one thermometer near the bowl.

Use clay under the bowl to hold it in place.

3 **Measure** and record the temperatures after 1 minute and after 3 minutes.

### Explain Your Results

1. Compare the effects of sunlight on the 2 thermometers.

2. **Infer** What caused the temperatures to be different?

# How to Read Science

## Cause and Effect

A **cause** is a reason something happens. An **effect** is what happens. A cause may have more than one effect. An effect may have more than one cause.

Sometimes your observations can also help you **make inferences** about what happened.

Read the following instructions in a handbook. Causes are highlighted in orange and effects are highlighted in blue.

**Camper's Handbook**

### Reflective Ovens

Can you bake cookies using energy from the Sun? The answer is yes. A reflective oven can be used to collect the Sun's energy. You can make a simple reflective oven from cardboard and foil. The shiny side of the foil should face out so that the sunlight will be reflected onto the cookies. The heat from the sunlight causes the cookies to bake. A reflective oven does not get as hot as a regular oven, so the cookies will take longer to bake. The cookies will still taste great!

## Apply It!

Complete a graphic organizer like the one shown by **making inferences** and by using the **causes** and **effects** in the article.

Cause → Effect

# You Are There!

You're walking with your class in the forest. It's pretty dark in the shady areas. Sunlight strikes the trees, but it hardly reaches the ground. Sunlight is a resource on which the forest—and all living things—depend. But there are many other important resources here too. You're walking on one of them right now! What are resources and why are they important?

AudioText

# What are natural resources?

*Living and nonliving things support life on Earth. Soil is an important renewable resource. So is the solar energy that we capture and use.*

## How Resources Are Used

Are you wearing jeans? Are you holding a pencil? Do you have an apple in your lunch? Have you sipped some water today? You're using natural resources! We use natural resources to make products and to provide energy.

Natural resources are supplies that nature provides. Living things, such as fungi, plants, and animals, are natural resources. So are nonliving things such as water, soil, minerals, sunlight, and other sources of energy. Take a deep breath. You just used another natural resource—air.

All living things depend on natural resources. Plants need air, sunlight, soil, and water to live. People need air and water too. They use plant and animal resources for food. Earth's resources also provide the raw materials that we use to make the products we need. Everything we eat, use, or buy has been made from or is a natural resource.

## Renewable Natural Resources

Earth has two types of natural resources, renewable and nonrenewable. Renewable resources can be replaced. **Solar energy,** which is energy the Sun gives off, is one renewable resource. Other renewable natural resources are water, oxygen in the air, trees in a forest, and soil in which food grows.

1.　✔Checkpoint　What are three natural resources?
2.　Writing in Science　**Narrative** Write a **science journal** entry that tells how you use natural resources in your daily activities.

**287**

## Why Soil Is a Renewable Resource

A big clump of dirt is actually an important renewable resource—soil. Soil covers most of Earth's land surface. Many animals, such as chipmunks, rabbits, and woodchucks, make their homes in soil. Trees and other plants need soil to live, too. The plants and animals provide food for other animals, including people. Like water, soil is a nonliving natural resource that Earth renews.

## How Soil Is Renewed

The processes of weathering, erosion, and deposition work together to form soil. Over time, loose rock that is at Earth's surface takes a beating. Water that drips into cracks in the rock freezes and thaws again and again. Ice pushing against the sides makes the cracks in the rock get larger. As the cracks get larger, the rock gets weaker. Eventually bits of the rock break apart. Wind containing rock and sand particles slowly scrubs away bits of loose rock.

Water breaks apart rock beneath Earth's surface too. Plant roots also force their way into rock and break it into smaller pieces. Over millions of years, this natural Earth process known as weathering wears down even the tallest mountains. Then, erosion deposits the weathered pieces in a new place.

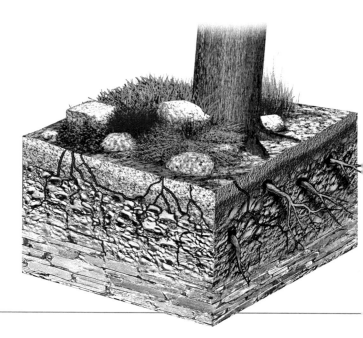

## Ingredients in Soil

Pieces of different kinds of weathered rock are a key ingredient in soil. Soil is full of other things too, such as decaying plant and animal remains. The decomposing material called **humus** is a rich dark brown color. Air and minerals are nonliving ingredients in soil. But as you can see in the picture above, soil is also full of life! Certain burrowing animals such as prairie dogs build elaborate towns underground. Tiny organisms such as bacteria, fungi, worms, spiders, and insects make their homes in soil. They break down the plant and animal remains into nutrients that plants can use as food.

Different soils are made from different kinds of rocks and minerals. How much humus is in the soil also affects the way it feels when you touch it. The minerals that are in the soil may affect its color. Soil samples that are taken just a few kilometers apart can look and feel very different!

1. ✔Checkpoint What are three key ingredients in soil?
2. Social Studies in Science In which region of the United States do you live? Find out about the types of soil that are often found in your region. Write about them in your **science journal.**

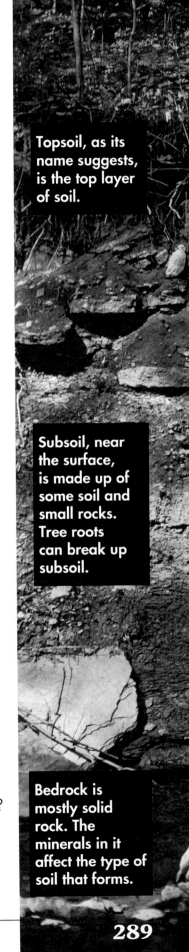

Topsoil, as its name suggests, is the top layer of soil.

Subsoil, near the surface, is made up of some soil and small rocks. Tree roots can break up subsoil.

Bedrock is mostly solid rock. The minerals in it affect the type of soil that forms.

## Properties of Soil

Each type of soil has certain qualities. Topsoil contains rotting plant and animal materials. It also has particles of weathered rock. Remember that ice, water, and decomposing animals and plants cause rock to weather. As rock weathers, it breaks into particles of various sizes.

*Clay*

## Clay, Silt, and Sand

Clay soil is made mostly of the very smallest particles. Clay may be different colors because of the materials in it. Clay with iron particles looks red, for example. Some clay feels sticky. Soil with slightly larger particles is called silt. Most particles in silty soil are slightly larger than those in clay. Silt particles feel smooth. Soil with still larger particles is called sand. Sandy soil contains particles from different materials. The most common mineral in sand is quartz. Sand may also contain feldspar or other minerals. Broken shells are in sand that is near oceans. Like other soils, the color of sand depends upon the materials in it. Some sand is very light colored. Sand that forms from mostly volcanic rock can be black.

*Silt*

*Sand*

Look at the close-ups of clay, silt, and sand. What differences do you notice? How do you think each would feel if you touched it?

## Soil for Growing Plants

Plants grow best in soil that has many nutrients. But, if the soil has too much sand or too much clay, plants are not able to soak up the nutrients. For example, water runs right through sandy soil, taking nutrients with it! Clay can hold lots of water, but it is so hard that plant roots can't spread very easily. Good soil for plants is the right mix of clay, silt, sand, and humus.

Adobe bricks made from soil harden in the Sun.

## Soil as a Renewable Natural Resource

Soil is renewable. Good farming can replace its nutrients naturally. Farmers can plant certain crops that put nutrients back into the soil. Plants that are plowed under also add nutrients and organic material to the soil. But, the soil itself takes longer to replace. Only a few centimeters of the rich topsoil layer are renewed every 1,000 years. That's slow—especially since a few centimeters of topsoil can wear away in just ten years. Conserving soil is important to all of us. Many groups are working to reduce soil erosion to protect this natural resource.

Jars made of clay have been used for centuries.

## Other Uses of Soil

When you think of soil, you may think of growing plants. You may think of the fertile silt in river sediment. But, soil can be used in other ways too. For example, clay is used to make tile, bricks, and pottery. When paper is being made, clay particles are sometimes added to make it strong and shiny. Sand is used as a raw material for making concrete, glass, and other things.

✅ **Lesson Checkpoint**

1. Soil is a renewable resource. What keeps it from renewing quickly?
2. **Cause and Effect** How do the amounts of sand, silt, and clay in soil affect plant growth?

## Lesson 2

# How are resources used for energy?

*Almost all of the energy we use is from the Sun. We also use the powerful forces of wind and moving water for energy. The Sun, wind, and moving water are sources of renewable energy.*

Solar cells have generated electricity for NASA.

## Renewable Energy Sources

Green plants need sunlight for photosynthesis. The solar energy is transferred to animals through the food chain. Animals use chemical energy stored in plants they eat.

People use energy in many ways too. We use it to run machines, heat our homes, and help grow our food. Solar energy is a renewable energy source. Sometimes we use the Sun's energy without knowing it. How does sunlight streaming through windows change the temperature of a room?

Solar energy affects Earth's temperatures. Sunlight warms Earth. Then the air that is closest to Earth's surface is heated when it touches the warm ground. The cycle of heating and cooling the air creates wind energy. Energy from the Sun powers the water cycle by causing water to evaporate.

Fields of solar panels absorb energy from the Sun and convert it into electricity.

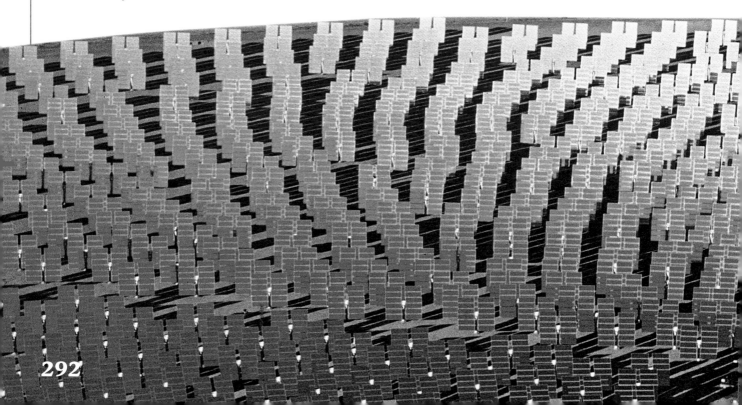

## How We Use Solar Energy

Is your calculator or watch solar powered? Inside your solar-powered device is a **solar cell** that changes energy from the Sun into electrical energy. Groups of solar cells form solar panels. Solar energy can be changed to electric energy to do many big jobs too. It is used to power satellites. On solar farms, fields of solar panels collect the Sun's energy. The solar energy can be changed into electric energy or into heat energy.

In a solar heat system, for example, the Sun's energy heats the water that flows through the solar panels. The heated water is stored in a tank until a pump forces it into a system of pipes. The piped water can then be used to heat homes and for activities, such as washing clothes. What are some other possible uses?

### Wind Energy
Wind is a source of renewable energy. Wind energy has been used for thousands of years. Windmills can be used to run machinery, pump water, and produce electric power.

## Energy from Flowing Water

Water flows from a high place to a lower place. Long ago, people built water wheels to use falling water to do work. They knew that moving water has energy. Today, people use the energy in flowing water to power the machines that produce electricity. In some places, dams are built to control the flow of water. Water is stored in a lake that forms behind the dam. The water is released when its energy is needed.

1. ✓**Checkpoint** How do we capture and use solar energy?
2. **Writing in Science** **Persuasive** Suppose your school district is building a new school. List reasons why the school should use solar power. Use your list to write a letter to a local newspaper to persuade readers to share your view.

Millions of years ago, swamps covered the land.

Thick layers of dead plants were buried. Over years and years, the layers hardened into sedimentary rock.

Now we remove the coal that formed.

## Nonrenewable Energy Sources

Nonrenewable resources are supplies that exist in limited amounts or are used much faster than they can be replaced in nature. People use ores and other nonrenewable resources to make products and to provide energy. An **ore** is a rock rich in minerals that can be removed from the Earth. Nonrenewable mineral resources are commonly found in ores.

## Fossil Fuels

Coal, natural gas, and oil are some nonrenewable energy sources. They are fuels, which means that they are burned to produce useful heat. Coal, natural gas, and oil are called **fossil fuels** because they were made from organisms that lived long ago. Do you realize that all the energy stored in fossil fuels can be traced to the Sun? It's true!

Oil is the everyday name for **petroleum.** Fossil fuels such as petroleum are the products of organisms that lived in the sea long ago. The bacteria, algae, and other organisms changed the energy in sunlight to produce energy to help them live. Their bodies stored whatever energy they didn't use. After they died, their remains and the unused stored energy settled on the seabed.

As more and more organisms settled, thick layers called sediments formed. Over millions of years, pressure from the weight of the upper layers squeezed the lower layers. The pressure, heat, and decaying action of the bacteria gradually changed the energy-rich remains. The chemicals stored in the bodies of these tiny organisms became oil and other fossil fuels.

## Impact of Fossil Fuels

Mining fossil fuels can harm the environment. Some of the richest oil deposits in the world are under the ocean floor. Getting to the oil can be risky.

The chance of an oil spill is one of the greatest dangers of drilling deep under the ocean. Oil spills cause pollution and other serious problems that kill marine organisms. Spills can also kill or harm plants and animals that live along coasts. Companies are working on ways to reduce the damage that might result from drilling and spills.

Using fossil fuels also has harmful effects. When fossil fuels burn, different substances are released into the air. Smoke and particles of ash, for example, make air unhealthy for living things to breathe. Increasing the amount of carbon dioxide gas in the atmosphere may lead to global warming. Sometimes gases break up in rainwater and create a weak acid. The acid falls to Earth in rain. This rain can damage buildings and harm plant and animal life on land and in water.

Offshore oil rigs tap into petroleum deposits that are deep beneath the ocean floor.

1. ✔Checkpoint How are Earth's resources reduced?
2. ⟳ Cause and Effect What are some possibly harmful results from using fossil fuels?

## How Resources Can Last Longer

For many years, the world has used nonrenewable resources to meet most of its energy needs. As people need more and more energy, fossil fuels will be used up faster and faster. Fuel costs will rapidly increase.

Fresh water, air, soil, and trees are resources that help all living things. But like Earth's nonrenewable resources, they will be reduced if we use them wastefully or destroy them on purpose or by accident. Restoring soil, forests, or fishing areas can be very difficult and costly! Cleaning up polluted air, water, and soil is expensive.

We can conserve energy to help our fossil fuels last longer. But, we should also try to use solar energy, wind power, water power, and other renewable energy sources.

Old tires can be used in construction, for fences, and for crash cushions. They can be used to make equipment for sports and playgrounds.

## Methods of Energy Conservation

**Conservation** means using only what you need as efficiently as possible. You can reduce energy use in many ways. For example, to travel a short distance, you can walk or ride a bike. For longer distances, you can share rides with others. Turn off lights that you don't need, and do not leave water taps running. Use what you need, and then shut the water off!

Energy-efficient cars and appliances use less energy to do the same amount of work. Less energy is used to heat and cool buildings with good insulation. Conserving energy will help our supply of fossil fuels last longer.

Some plastics are melted, shredded, formed, and recycled into T-shirts, quilted jackets, and sleeping bags!

The rubber in old tires can be ground up into small pieces called crumb rubber. The crumb rubber is added to the mixture that is used to pave roads and airport runways.

## Recycling

**Recycling** is saving, collecting, or using materials again instead of treating them as waste. Some products and materials are easier to recycle than others. Glass, cardboard, newspaper, paper, aluminum, tin, steel, and some plastics can be recycled. You may have noticed a symbol marked on plastic objects that can be recycled. The recycling symbol looks like three arrows chasing each other around a triangle. A number inside the triangle tells what materials were used to make the kind of plastic in the object.

Many products that are made from natural resources should be recycled! Paper comes from wood. Plastics come from petroleum. And glass is made from sand. Many cans are made from aluminum, which is made from an ore. More than half of the aluminum cans sold are recycled. By recycling, we can reuse raw materials.

Many items made of steel or aluminum can be recycled.

Is your notepad made of recycled paper? Used paper can be recycled into new paper!

Ground glass can replace sand in concrete.

✔ **Lesson Checkpoint**

1. How can we conserve energy?
2. **Writing in Science** **Persuasive** Create a poster to persuade students in your grade to conserve energy.

## Investigate How can you observe a "fossil fuel" being formed?

Natural gas, a type of fossil fuel, can form when some materials decay.

### Materials

2 liter plastic bottle with meat (prepared by teacher)

4 lettuce leaves

funnel, graduated cylinder, water

sand

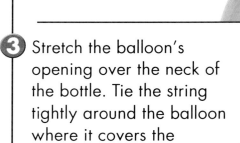

small balloon, string, tape

### Process Skills

**Making a model** of a process can help you understand what happens when the process occurs in nature.

### What to Do

① Tear 4 lettuce leaves into small pieces. Add them to the bottle with meat. Pour 40 mL of sand over them. Do not shake the bottle.

*Use the funnel when measuring the sand, when adding the sand, and when adding the water.*

② Pour 20 mL of water into the bottle so it runs down the side in the bottle.

③ Stretch the balloon's opening over the neck of the bottle. Tie the string tightly around the balloon where it covers the bottle's neck.

④ Put tape over the string and around the edge of the balloon to seal it to the bottle.

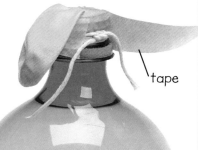

tape

**5** Put the bottle in a warm place for 5 days. Each day observe the balloon and the contents of the bottle. Try to detect *any* change. Record what you observe. You have made a **model** of the process of decay.

Natural gas should be produced very slowly. The balloon will not expand, but after 5 days enough natural gas may have been produced to cause the balloon to stand straight up.

Be careful!

Wash your hands when finished.

| Day | Balloon | Contents of Bottle |
|-----|---------|--------------------|
| Day 1 | | |
| Day 2 | | |
| Day 3 | | |
| Day 4 | | |
| Day 5 | | |

## Explain Your Results

1. Did the balloon and the contents of the bottle change? How?
2. **Infer** What made the balloon change?

### Go Further

What would happen to the formation of natural gas if you changed the conditions, such as the temperature or the amount of water? Make a plan to find out.

# Water Use

Water is a renewable natural resource. But, did you know just how renewable it is? Nearly every single drop of water we use trickles back to a lake, sea, or ocean. The Sun's heat causes water to evaporate and then return to Earth in the form of rain, snow, sleet, or hail. This cycle goes on and on—so water is never used up! But that doesn't mean it's OK for us to use it carelessly.

The circle graph shows how much water an average American family of four uses each day in three different rooms. The average household uses about 1,150 liters of water per day.

## Daily Water Use

Laundry: 140 L

Kitchen: 125 L

Bathroom: 885 L

**1** In which location is the greatest amount of water used?
A. kitchen
B. dining room
C. laundry area
D. bathroom

**2** How much water does the average American household use each week?
F. 8,050 liters
G. 770 liters
H. 157 liters
I. 77 liters

**3** In a family of four, about how much water does each person use per day?
A. 4,600 liters
B. 2,870 liters
C. 287 liters
D. 28.7 liters

**4** How much more water is used in the bathroom each day than in the kitchen and laundry combined?
F. 885 liters
G. 620 liters
H. 265 liters
I. 125 liters

## Lab zone Take-Home Activity

For one day, estimate the amount of water you use in the bathroom at home. Use a timer and the table below to help you. If your family has information about the water usage of your sink, shower, and toilet, use those figures instead of those in the table.

| Fixture | Average Water Used |
|---------|-------------------|
| Sink | 11 liters per minute |
| Shower | 8 liters per minute |
| Toilet Flushing | 12 liters per flush |

# Chapter 10 Review and Test Prep

## Use Vocabulary

| | |
|---|---|
| **conservation** (p. 296) | **recycling** (p. 297) |
| **fossil fuels** (p. 294) | **solar cells** (p. 293) |
| **humus** (p. 289) | **solar energy** (p. 287) |
| **ore** (p. 294) | |
| **petroleum** (p. 294) | |

Use the term from the list above that best completes each sentence.

1. To use only what you need as efficiently as possible is _____.

2. To save, collect, or use materials again instead of treating them as waste is _____.

3. The energy given off by the Sun is _____.

4. A nonrenewable energy source also known as oil is _____.

5. Fuels made from the remains of living things that died millions of years ago are _____.

6. The dark brown part of soil made up of rotting plants and animals is _____.

7. A mineral-rich rock deposit that can be removed from the Earth is _____.

8. _____ convert the Sun's energy into electricity.

## Explain Concepts

9. The Sun is the major source of energy on Earth. Explain how all living things capture and use the Sun's energy.

10. Explain why our need for fossil fuels can harm the environment.

### Process Skills

11. **Collect Data** Conserve with your class! Figure out how many sheets of paper you dispose of in one week. Then try to reduce, reuse, or recycle. Collect data over a three-week period. Compare the before-and-after figures in a diagram, chart, graph, or drawing.

12. **Make Observations** The Environmental Protection Agency estimates that 1 billion juice boxes are thrown away each year. Using what you observe in your classroom, develop a plan that your class could use to reduce that number.

##  Cause and Effect

**13.** When we misuse our natural resources, we can affect all living things. Copy the graphic organizer below. Complete it by adding four causes that might lead to the effect that is given.

| Cause | → | Effect |
|-------|---|--------|
|       |   | Harmful things happen to plants, animals, and people. |

## Test Prep

Choose the letter that best completes the statement.

**14.** A nonrenewable natural resource is
Ⓐ coal.
Ⓑ soil.
Ⓒ oxygen.
Ⓓ trees.

**15.** Subsoil is mostly made up of
Ⓕ solar energy.
Ⓖ petroleum.
Ⓗ small rocks.
Ⓘ solid rock.

**16.** The smallest particles of sediments are found in
Ⓐ humus.
Ⓑ silt.
Ⓒ sand.
Ⓓ clay.

**17.** All of the energy that is stored in fossil fuels can be traced to
Ⓕ the Sun.
Ⓖ humus.
Ⓗ swamps.
Ⓘ offshore drilling.

**18.** Coal that has formed over millions of years can be traced back to organisms living in
Ⓐ silt, sand, and clay.
Ⓑ eroded soil.
Ⓒ swamps.
Ⓓ strip mines.

**19.** Explain why your answer for Question 14 is the best choice. For each answer you did not select, give a reason why it is not the best choice.

**20.** **Writing** in Science **Descriptive**
Suppose you have invented a machine that runs on energy sources from the Sun, wind, or moving water. Write a paragraph that describes what your invention does. Don't forget to tell what it looks like and how it uses renewable energy.

# Auto Engineer

Would you like to build a car that uses renewable energy? You could become part of a team that designs a solar-powered car. The United States Department of Energy sponsors the American Solar Challenge (ASC). The ASC is a solar car competition. Students from colleges and universities in the United States and Canada design solar-powered cars and race them across the country.

The students work in teams. The teams put their cars through vigorous tests and inspections to be sure they are safe. Then the race is on!

The solar cars are flashy, but they have some problems. They seat only one or two people. There's not much space to carry things, and, as you may have guessed, they run only during the day! Even so, solar cars help us learn more about solar energy and how it can be used.

Most of the students who build the cars are mainly studying science, math, and engineering. Many will become mechanical engineers and design other kinds of cars or find other ways to use solar energy. They study in colleges or universities for four or more years to get a degree in engineering.

## Lab zone Take-Home Activity

Hybrid vehicles can use two or more different kinds of power. Use the Internet or other sources to learn about vehicles that use both solar power and another source of energy.

# Unit B Test Talk

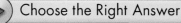
## Choose the Right Answer

To answer a multiple-choice test question, you need to choose an answer from several choices. Read the passage and then answer the questions.

Although precipitation falls all over Earth, most of it falls into the oceans. Rain is the most common form of precipitation. Sometimes raindrops pass through a layer of cold air as they fall from a cloud to the ground. If the temperature of the air is colder than 0°C, the raindrops freeze into small pieces of ice, called sleet. If the pieces are larger than 5 mm across, the little balls of ice are called hailstones.

As a hailstone begins its trip toward the ground, strong winds may carry it back up into colder air. When it starts to fall again, the winds may carry it up a second time. Each time the hailstone moves back into a colder region of the cloud, another layer of ice is added to it. This cycle may repeat many times before the hailstone becomes so heavy that it falls to the ground. If you cut a hailstone in half, you can see rings of ice. Each ring represents an up-and-down trip through the cloud.

Like snow and sleet, hail is the result of moisture that freezes. But most hailstorms occur in summer! Hail is formed in the same type of clouds that produce thunderstorms, and thunderstorms usually happen in warm weather.

## Use What You Know

In order to choose the right answer, you might first eliminate answer choices that you are sure are incorrect. As you read each question, decide which answer choice you can eliminate.

1. In which month is a hailstorm most likely to occur in the United States?
   Ⓐ December
   Ⓑ February
   Ⓒ June
   Ⓓ November

2. When a hailstone is cut in half, you see
   Ⓕ rings of ice.
   Ⓖ a snowflake.
   Ⓗ a small pebble.
   Ⓘ a raindrop.

3. Hail and snow are similar because
   Ⓐ both are common in cold weather.
   Ⓑ both happen in hot climates.
   Ⓒ both form when moisture freezes.
   Ⓓ both form in temperatures warmer than 0°C.

4. Most precipitation falls in the form of
   Ⓕ hailstones.
   Ⓖ rain.
   Ⓗ sleet.
   Ⓘ snow.

# Unit B Wrap-Up

## Chapter 6

### How does Earth's water affect weather?
- The water cycle changes salty ocean water into the fresh water we need for our daily activities.
- Weather depends on the way air masses move and interact.
- Scientists use many measurements to predict the weather.

## Chapter 7

### How do storms affect Earth's air, water, land, and living things?
- A hurricane is formed by bands of strong thunderstorms swirling around an area of calm.
- Tornadoes are violent, swirling winds that can appear with little warning.

## Chapter 8

### How can rocks tell us about Earth's past, present, and future?
- Rocks are classified by how they formed.
- Fossils in rock are clues to Earth's past.

## Chapter 9

### How is Earth's surface shaped and reshaped?
- Erosion and deposition of weathered rock change landforms over long periods of time.
- Volcanoes, earthquakes, and other natural forces change Earth's surface quickly.

# Chapter 10

### How can living things always have the resources they need?

- Natural resources are both living and nonliving.
- Some natural resources are renewable, and some are not.
- Some sources of energy are renewable, and some are not.

## Performance Assessment

### Wind Vane

Make a wind vane. Make sure that whatever materials you use are sturdy enough to last in the wind. You want to make especially sure that the pointer turns but does not bend. Take your wind vane outside. Use it to determine the direction of the wind. Describe how you made the wind vane and how it showed the direction of the wind.

## Read More About Earth Science

Look for books such as these in the library.

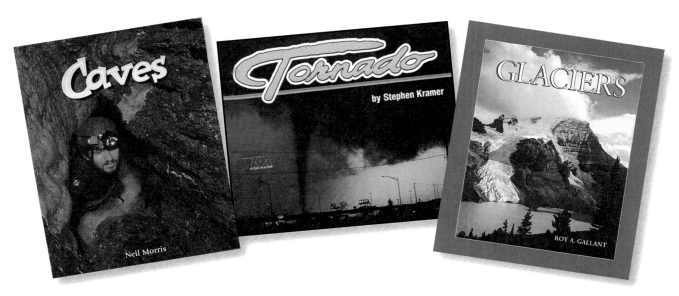

# Lab zone Full Inquiry

## Experiment What affects how rain erodes soil?

Moving water can change the land.
It can carry soil from one place to another.

### Materials

gloves and masking tape

3 containers and soil

small paper cup and 3 books

small paper clip
and foam cup

water and
graduated cylinder
(or measuring cup)

metric ruler

### Process Skills

Scientists
sometimes make
**estimates**
when exact
**measurements**
are not needed.

### Ask a question.

How does the way water falls on soil change the
amount of soil the water moves?

### State a hypothesis.

You will conduct 2 experiments. You will make
and test 2 hypotheses. Scientists sometimes
conduct 2 experiments together. Why do you
think they do so?

If more water falls on soil, then will more,
less, or about the same amount of soil be eroded?
Write your **hypothesis**.

If water falls on soil faster, then will more,
less, or about the same amount of soil be eroded?
Write your hypothesis.

### Identify and control variables.

In these **experiments**, the variable you
observe is the amount of soil the water moves.
Other conditions, such as the slope of the soil,
the amount of soil, and the type of soil, must stay
the same. Water is the **variable** you will change.
In one test you use more water (container B). In a
second test you let the water fall faster (container C).
You compare both with the control (container A).

## Test your hypothesis.

**1** Empty 1 small paper cup of soil into one end of each container. Put a book under each container to raise the end with the soil.

**Be careful!**

Wear gloves.

Label the containers A, B, and C.

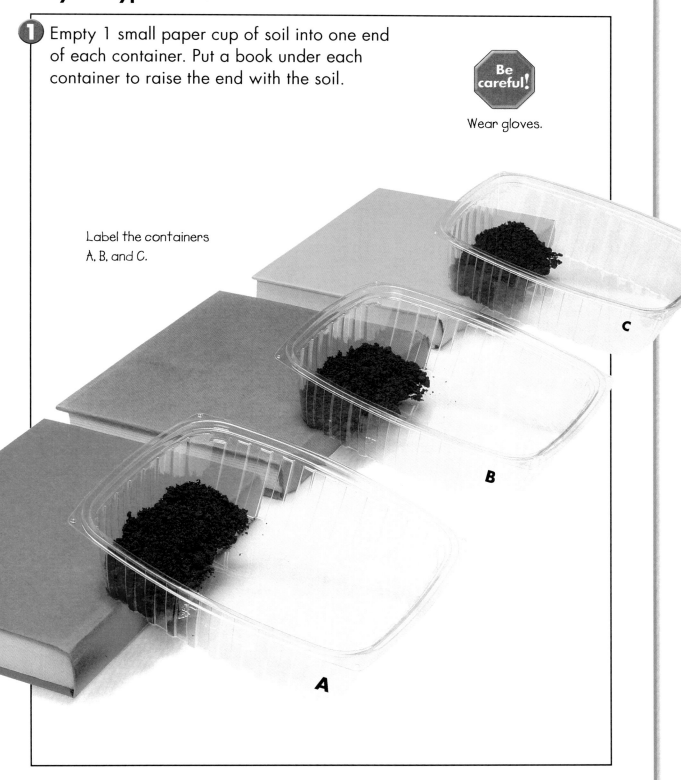

C

B

A

**2** **Measure** 50 mL of water with a graduated cylinder. Unbend the end of a small paper clip. Use the tip to poke 2 small holes in the bottom of a foam cup. Hold the cup 6 cm above the soil in container A. Pour the water into the cup with holes. Let it drip onto the soil.

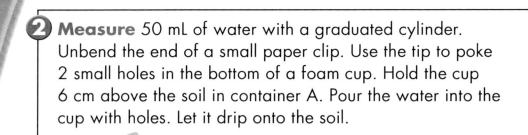

**3** Let 100 mL of water drip from the cup onto the soil in container B.

**4** Use the paper clip to make the holes in the cup 3 times as wide. Let 50 mL of water pour from the cup onto the soil in container C.

6 cm

A

**5** **Observe** the soil in each container. How has it changed? Record your **observations** in the chart. **Estimate** the fraction of the soil that was moved, or eroded.

## Collect and record your data.

| Container | Amount of Water Added (mL) | Amount of Erosion Observed (Estimate the fraction of the soil that moved.) |
|---|---|---|
| **Container A** (control) | | |
| **Container B** (more water) | | |
| **Container C** (faster water) | | |

## Interpret your data.

Analyze your data. Make circle graphs to show your data. Explain your data to another group. Compare your data with the data from other groups.

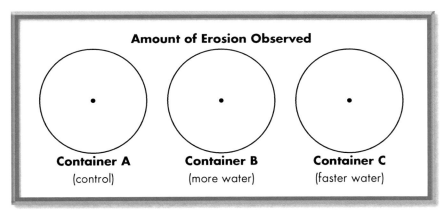

**Amount of Erosion Observed**

Container A (control)   Container B (more water)   Container C (faster water)

For each circle graph, find the fraction of soil that was eroded. Then shade in that fraction of the circle.

## State your conclusion.

Remember that you conducted 2 experiments. Think about your first hypothesis. What conclusion can you draw from your chart? Does it agree with your hypothesis? **Communicate** your conclusion. Repeat for your second hypothesis.

## Go Further

You observed how soil was eroded. Would your results change if you tested sand, mud, or rocks instead? How would changing the slope of the soil affect your results? Design and carry out a plan to investigate these or other questions you may have.

### Using Scientific Methods
1. Ask a question.
2. State a hypothesis.
3. Identify and control variables.
4. Test your hypothesis.
5. Collect and record your data.
6. Interpret your data.
7. State your conclusion.
8. Go further.

### The Answer Is Blowing in the Wind

**Idea:** Design and conduct an experiment to see if wind conditions affect the rate of evaporation from a body of water. Be sure to have adult supervision if you use an electric fan when you complete your experiment. Write a summary to explain the results of your experiment.

### Acid Rain

**Idea:** Test what effect acid rain has on buildings and statues. Place a piece of chalk in a cup of water. Place an identical piece of chalk in a cup of vinegar. (Vinegar is an acid.) After 24 hours, compare the pieces of chalk. Infer what effect acid rain has on materials such as limestone and marble that are similar to chalk.

### Please Pass the Salt Water

**Idea:** Use the Internet or other sources to research ways to remove the salt from seawater. Use your research to design a way to make fresh water from salt water by either evaporation and condensation or by freezing.

### The Last Straw

**Idea:** Model how ice can weather rock. Freeze a drinking straw that you've filled with water. The next day, remove it from the freezer. Write a summary to explain what happened and why.